ALL ABOUT
UFOs

By Jonathan Rutland

Designed by David Nash

Edited by Katie Cohen

Illustrators

Roger Full • Roger Payne

Ron Jobson • Brian Pearce

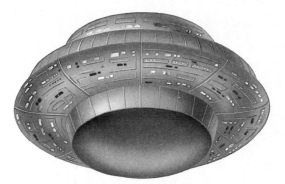

NUTMEG PRESS

This edition published by Nutmeg Press
(A Division of Shelley Graphics Ltd.)
Printed in the United States
ISBN 0-89943-116-X

CONTENTS

The best known type of unidentified flying object is the "flying saucer." In 1967 a barber in Ohio claimed to have photographed one which had been hovering over his house.

The UFO Story

The letters UFO stand for Unidentified Flying Object. UFOs are mysterious flying things. If we knew what they were, they would be IFOs — Identified Flying Objects. An aircraft is an IFO. So are satellites, kites, balloons and meteors, all commonly mistaken for UFOs.

Many people think that every UFO sighting *must* have an ordinary explanation, even though it is not always possible to find one. Others believe that UFOs do exist and cannot readily be explained away. The popular idea is that UFOs, if they exist, come from space.

Through the centuries, people have observed unusual objects in the sky. From about 1950 these stories were given much publicity in newspapers. The number of reports grew and grew. Many were hoaxes. Many turned out to be distant stars or planets. But there were always a few unsolved mysteries.

Throughout the world, organizations sprang up to investigate UFOs. But despite their research we are still unsure whether to be excited, or afraid, or whether we should just laugh about UFOs.

In September 1976 a UFO appeared over Iran. Two Phantom jet fighters approached it and both found that all weapons, radios and instruments jammed when close to the UFO. It even appeared to fire a missile at one of the jets.

In 1861 observers at the Radcliffe Observatory in Oxford, England, saw a UFO. They said it was a glowing light which moved around the sky, stopping and changing direction several times.

The Socorro Saucer

This is one of the most famous stories involving an encounter with a UFO. It happened in New Mexico, on the afternoon of April 24, 1964. A police officer called Lonnie Zamora was chasing a speeding car in Socorro County when he heard a roar and saw a blue flame in the sky. The flaming ball was slowly coming down not far away.

Zamora pulled off the road and went to investigate. He spotted an oval silvery-white object. Standing nearby were two human-looking beings about the size of ten-year-old children.

He drove closer to the object, and radioed to his headquarters. Then he stopped and got out of the car. By this time the "humanoid" creatures had re-entered the craft. There was a slam which sounded like a hatch closing, followed by an ear-splitting roar.

Zamora was terrified and ran back toward the car. He tripped and fell and on glancing back he saw the UFO taking off to the southwest. It sped silently away. Later, investigators found strange burn marks on the ground where the craft had stood.

Illusions and Frauds

Ufologists are people who study UFOs. When they receive a UFO sighting report their first task is to check it carefully to see if the object can be identified. Often there is a simple explanation. All the objects pictured here could be mistaken for UFOs. The strange clouds above look very like flying saucers. They are called lenticular clouds because of their lens shape.

Aircraft are sometimes mistaken for UFOs, particularly when the landing lights flash. The ufologist must check what aircraft were in the sky at the time of the UFO report.

UFOs are most often seen at

These odd lights are caused by a strange and rare kind of lightning called ball lightning.

The car is out of sight, but its lights show up in the fog, and can be mistaken for UFOs.

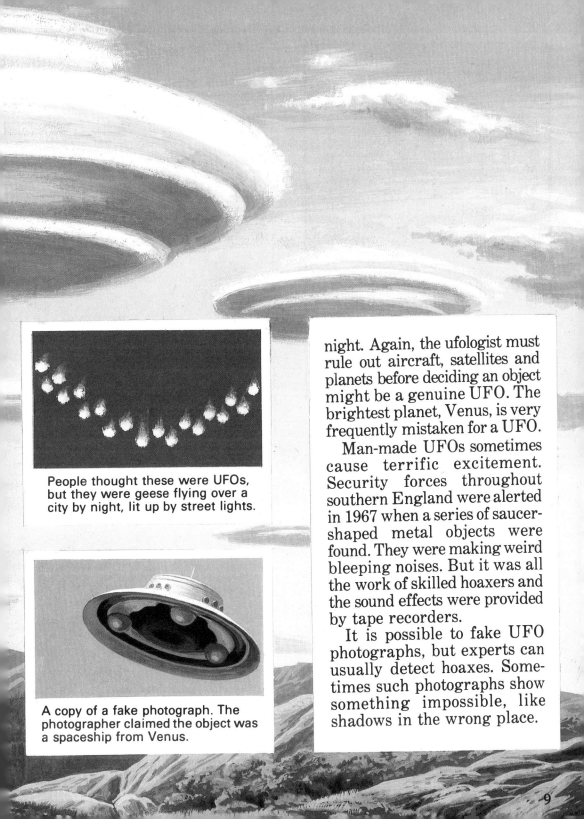

People thought these were UFOs, but they were geese flying over a city by night, lit up by street lights.

A copy of a fake photograph. The photographer claimed the object was a spaceship from Venus.

night. Again, the ufologist must rule out aircraft, satellites and planets before deciding an object might be a genuine UFO. The brightest planet, Venus, is very frequently mistaken for a UFO.

Man-made UFOs sometimes cause terrific excitement. Security forces throughout southern England were alerted in 1967 when a series of saucer-shaped metal objects were found. They were making weird bleeping noises. But it was all the work of skilled hoaxers and the sound effects were provided by tape recorders.

It is possible to fake UFO photographs, but experts can usually detect hoaxes. Sometimes such photographs show something impossible, like shadows in the wrong place.

9

Close Encounters

UFO sightings at close quarters are now referred to as close encounters. The term was coined by a scientist, Dr. J. Allen Hynek, who was adviser to the official U.S. Air Force UFO investigation. At first a non-believer, he found that the genuine mystery behind some UFO reports was convincing.

A close encounter of the first kind is a sighting of a UFO which is fairly close. There is no contact with the UFO and it does not land.

In a close encounter of the

These are pictures of photographs showing UFOs in close encounters of the first kind. Clear photographs are very rare, partly because most UFOs are seen at night.

A close encounter of the second kind. A UFO left a circular mark on the ground. Later snow fell. Then the snow melted, but it did not thaw on the UFOs mark until much later.

second kind there are physical traces of the UFO as well as a sighting. For example, people have reported UFOs causing their car engines and lights to fail. If the UFO lands it may scorch the ground or leave prints made by its weight.

The most exciting and extraordinary UFO sighting is a close encounter of the third kind, for living creatures are seen in or near the UFO. Some of them seem to be grotesque little goblins. However most reports say the creatures are like humans, that they are intelligent, but with peculiar skin and clothing.

A close encounter of the third kind. Many witnesses have described the "ufonauts" (UFO occupants) they say they have seen. These are often like small human beings but with large heads.

Top Secret

Many people think that one possible explanation for UFOs is that they are secret weapons made by the United States or the U.S.S.R. This is most unlikely as such weapons would hardly be tested where they might be seen. And no one has yet built a craft that can suddenly change direction when traveling at very high speed. This is something UFOs seem to do often.

Some UFO enthusiasts think that our governments believe UFOs are from space, but that they do not want us to know. They think we might panic. It is a strange idea, for if we knew UFOs were from outer space, would we really be frightened and expect ufonauts to harm us? It is just as likely that people would be amazed and curious to hear about their world.

In 1938 there was a play on the radio called *War of the Worlds*. It was by the writer H. G. Wells, and was broadcast in New York. The play was about people from Mars making war on our world. Many listeners thought they were listening to the news. What happened is shown below. People ran out into the streets in panic. They were terrified, rushing around looking for the Martians who they thought intended to kill them. Perhaps the same panic would occur if a UFO landed in a major city.

An experimental plane known as the "flying pancake" was tried out by the U.S. Navy in the 1940's. Seen from below it would resemble a UFO.

Project Blue Book

In the 1950's, many people were excited and worried about UFOs. There were wild theories that they carried invaders from space, or from Russia. The U.S. Air Force investigation was stepped up and renamed Project Blue Book. Thousands of UFO sightings were investigated by the Project officers. About a quarter of the UFOs were satellites or meteors. Another quarter were stars or planets and many were planes or balloons. But there always remained some mysteries. Blue Book could not explain UFOs away.

The UFO Search

All kinds of different people are interested in UFOs, and the methods of searching for them vary widely.

Many keen amateur ufologists go out into the country to watch for UFOs. They are usually equipped with binoculars and cameras so that if they are lucky enough to see a UFO, they will try to photograph it, record its position, its movements, its size, color and shape and any other details. They are usually unlucky. UFOs do not seem to appear when one is looking for them.

Some places are particularly favored by UFO searchers because they have been the scenes of a number of UFO sightings. In the USA most sightings have been in the southeastern states, though sightings have occurred elsewhere.

Perhaps one day a group of UFO searchers will be lucky enough to have a close encounter like the one pictured on the far right. If they are able to photograph the craft and any occupants, it would provide proof that UFOs are real. At the moment we cannot be certain.

Because we do not know for certain what UFOs are, it is difficult to know how to obtain scientific facts about them. But there is an increasing number of scientists who are interested in UFOs. Their access to sensitive listening and recording devices may help provide new knowledge about these phenomena.

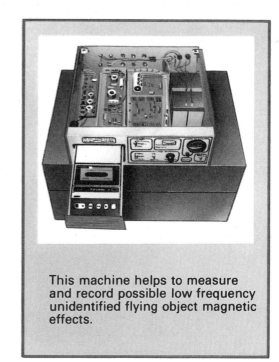

This machine helps to measure and record possible low frequency unidentified flying object magnetic effects.

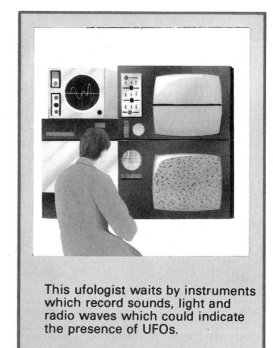

This ufologist waits by instruments which record sounds, light and radio waves which could indicate the presence of UFOs.

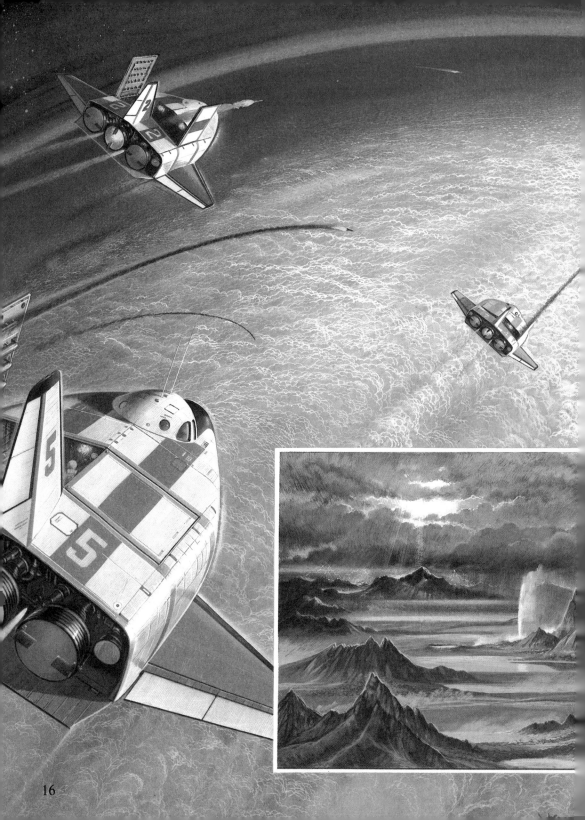

Earthly Flying Objects

Scientists have sent many strange-looking satellites into space, some of which are visible from the ground on a clear night. A large space satellite looks like a bright pinpoint of light silently gliding across the sky. It is easy to understand how spacecraft have been mistaken for UFOs.

One day manned spacecraft may be sent to the other planets in the solar system, probably to Venus, our nearest neighbor. As Venus orbits the sun more quickly than the Earth does, spacecraft would set out when Venus was behind the Sun and approach it as it neared the Earth. Scientists may even try to change the atmosphere of another planet, such as Venus, to make it possible for human beings to live there.

The Venusian atmosphere consists largely of hot carbon dioxide gas. There are few traces of oxygen, the gas all animals breathe, so no animal could survive there. But simple plants might be able to, for they thrive on carbon dioxide — and produce oxygen at the same time. In the large picture, spacecraft are "seeding" Venus with algae from Earth. These simple plants were among the earliest forms of life on Earth, and scientists believe that they are largely responsible for the oxygen in our atmosphere. Gradually the algae might change the atmosphere of Venus in the same way. As the algae consumed the hot carbon dioxide the atmosphere would cool down. Water vapor would start to condense and fall as rain. The new cooler surface of Venus should be able to support higher plants and animal life from Earth, and eventually human beings too.

Now try to imagine that some form of intelligent beings exists on a planet seeded by spaceships from Earth. Imagine that their world is not very advanced. They do not have radio or television. Nor do they have aircraft or spaceships. To them the spacecraft from Earth would be a complete mystery. They would be "unidentified flying objects." Perhaps our puzzlement and sense of mystery about UFOs reported on Earth means that they come from a more advanced world than ours.

In the future spacecraft might spread algae to transform the atmosphere of hot dry planets like Venus.

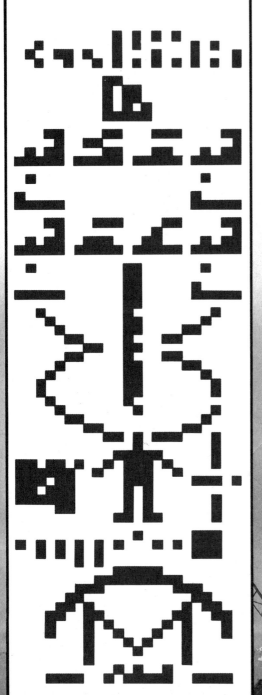

UFOs sometimes show up on radar screens. The arrow points to a "blip" typical of a UFO as seen on a radar screen.

Right: a time-lapse photograph showing the corkscrew path taken by a glowing UFO in the night sky.

Hello, Out There

The most exciting space probe to think about is *Pioneer 10,* sent up in early 1972. *Pioneer 10* is the first human-made object to go beyond our solar system. Its mission: to carry messages from earth to any intelligent beings who might be in outer space. When it passed Jupiter, *Pioneer 10* took more than 340 photographs. These were the first close-up shots of Jupiter. When near Jupiter, it reached speeds of 82,000 miles per hour.
Pioneer 10 now heads toward Pluto. It is expected to reach our farthest planet by 1987. After that, interstellar space! And who knows? It might greet some friendly alien beyond our solar system. Hello, out there!

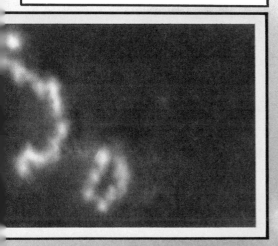

Huge radio telescopes like the one on the left can detect weak radio signals from outer space. They can also send out powerful signals toward far distant stars.

Radio Messages

Are there living creatures anywhere else in the universe? The question is of great concern to ufologists.

There are countless millions of stars in the universe: many must have planets orbiting them. Many astronomers think there must be life on some of them. The astronomers listen for radio messages from distant planets which might provide proof of life in space.

The problem is much worse than looking for a needle in a haystack. There are so many very distant stars and planets. Also the "people" of other worlds might be very different from us and they certainly would not speak our language. So what kind of messages might reach us from space and what signals should we send?

One answer is to use the "language" of computers. The computer message on the far left was sent out in 1974 to a group of stars in the constellation Hercules. It includes a "picture" of a human being and information on our solar system. However, the message will take 24,000 years to reach its destination so we should not expect a quick answer!

Spaceships

Astronauts have traveled from Earth to the Moon, and robot spacecraft have landed on Mars. But our present-day spacecraft are too slow to take astronauts to the more distant planets in the solar system. To reach the planets of other stars, where ufonauts might live, would take thousands of lifetimes.

One of the major problems of space travel is the enormous amount of energy needed to escape the Earth's gravity. Huge rockets are needed to launch even the smallest spacecraft. The solution is to build spacecraft in space where there is virtually no gravity. This is one reason why space stations such as *Skylab* (shown on the right) have been built.

Space stations of the future will circle high above the Earth. Engineers and materials will be flown to and from them in space shuttles — a mixture of spacecraft and airplane. One day enormous spaceships may be assembled and launched from space stations. But even hurtling through space at near the speed of light it would still take astronauts more than four years to reach the nearest star.

Voyager will send back to Earth information about the planets beyond the solar system.

Puzzles and Problems

Can UFOs really be spacecraft from other worlds? If so, where do they come from, and how do they get here?

Our closest neighbors in space are the other planets of our solar system. Astronomers do not think there is life on any of them. This means that UFOs would have to come from the planets of another star. It would take thousands of years for our present spacecraft to reach the nearest star. And most stars are much further away. Even if the ufonauts have spacecraft enormously faster than ours, the journey still seems impossibly long. Unless they have solved the secret of traveling faster than the speed of light — which Earthly science holds to be impossible.

Many ufologists, while believing that UFOs exist, do not think that they are interplanetary spacecraft at all. Some, for example, think that UFOs may be time travel machines and perhaps not material in the sense we understand it.

This theory would explain why no UFO has ever been captured. It would also explain why there are so many reports of UFOs which suddenly vanish into thin air.

If ufonauts come from other planets, why are they visiting Earth? If they would land and let us make contact with them all our questions could be answered.

There is also a widely held theory that UFOs come from universes around us which we cannot see. The illustration shows how a ghostly UFO might materialize on Earth from another universe. It would be a dramatic solution to the puzzles and problems of UFOs.

Glossary of Terms

Astronomy The scientific study of the heavenly bodies.

Close encounter A UFO sighting in which the UFO is usually less than 60 miles (100 km) away.

Computer An electronic brain. Computers are used to help control robot and manned spacecraft.

Flying saucer One of the first and best known names for UFOs.

Galaxy A collection of stars bound together by gravity.

Humanoid A UFO being similar to a human being, with a head, a body, two legs and two arms.

IFO An identified flying object.

Light year The distance light travels in one year. This is 5,878,000,000,000 miles (9,460,000,000,000 km).

Meteor A chunk of matter falling toward Earth from space. As it hurtles down it burns up in the Earth's atmosphere. All we see is a streak of light — a "shooting star." If it reaches the ground it is called a "meteorite."

Orbit Path of one body through space under the gravitational pull of another.

Planet A heavenly body which revolves around a star. The Earth is a planet.

Radio telescope A giant telescope studying radio waves instead of light.

Satellite Any body which orbits another bigger body. For example the Earth is a satellite of the Sun. Man-made satellites are used for communications purposes, and to gather information on the Earth and the weather.

Solar system The name for our Sun and its family of planets.

Star A huge fiery ball of gas in space. Our Sun is a star.

Ufonaut A member of the crew of a UFO.

Ufologist Someone who studies UFOs.

Universe All the matter, energy and space that exists — as far as we know.